ONE-SIDED FLIRTINSHIP

FROM DEAD TO ALIVE

GOURAV PALIWAL

To

My Love

Who always support me

in any situation but as a bestfriend.

Contents

Foreword

To readers,

I'm happy to express you the feelings which I got after reading the Book - "One-sided Flirtinship". According to me, you all must have to read this amazing book once in the life. In this Book, You all get some of the happy moments, sad moments, emotional attachments & many more.

The Chapters prepared with fully-focused mind & Great Technique of storytelling. Whenever, you read the book you relate it's chapters with your real life day-to-day activities. Poems of this Books must connect Us with our love.

I must referred you to read this book.

- QalamK Shokeen (Group)

Preface

Hey Everyone

Thank you to showing interest to read or purchase this book.

First of all, I'm thankful to my love who give me the idea of writing a book in an innovative manner. The Book - "One-sided Flirtinship" is all about my experience which I felt in my previous years. The Book is based on the real story of the author in the concept of Relationship. The Chapters have waves towards the writer's thought process as sometime he felt happy but in some moments he totally depressed from his life and loveone's. He express his love with the recitation of Poetries.

I must say to read this book at once because It's grow with many complications and confusions in the relationship of author & his love.

Happy to read.

Acknowledgements

The writer thanks to his family to support him, his friends to give this wonderful opportunity to write this book & the most important person of his life - His Love who guide him to write it no matter it's promote or not.

Prologue

Hey All

Let's see the trailor of the Book - "One-sided Flirtinship"

Here, The poet express his feeling via poetries which connect you with your loveone's. In first poem, He saw the love for the Lord Shiva on the occassion of Sawan. Then, He will dedicate his poetries to his love

Read the Poems & Comments on it

Let's Enjoy...

CHAPTER ONE

Mahadev

Before start this series of Poetry. Let's begin with Self-made Poetry of Lord Shiv or Mere Mahadev By Gourav Paliwal on the occassion of Sawan.

To my Mahadev
in Sawan bathed in water,
Mahadev by performing
Rudrabhishek blessing is received
Everyone says that sorrow
is the part of life
very unique essence
I say that Mahadev himself happy
life communication
you open your mind
he will remove the pain from the heart
If you sincerely demand then
he will show such a wonderful miracle
before the devotees
all you will get Seeing such glory,
the devotee again
Har Har Mahadev will shout.

CHAPTER TWO

My First Date

Before we start our amazing journey with this wonderful Book - "One-sided Flirtinship" with lots of Excitements. Let's enjoy the poetry - "My First Date" written by Gourav Paliwal.

"Here I tell something interested event in my Life
When first time I date a girl having cute smile
She never tried to cheat me at any point
of my lovely Life."
"The day is so beautiful and environment is too crazy
I am waiting for a call she will tell me the time
The phone rang and I run to pick up the
call, she said - Hello Gourav!"
"Oh! I really going to be shy away
She waiting of my reply
I said to her that
Yes, Hello!"
"Now I felt that she also going to be shy away
I am happy "she also felt what I too"
She said shall we meet today
at Dil Ek Pyaas Restro."
"The happiness on my face is going too high
Because the Restro is famous for love
Many Dates goes success at that

wonderful Restro."
"I am so excited and thought what should I talk with her
What she will ask from me and what's my answer
I really afraid about the situation and prays
To get the Relaxation."
"The time runs too slow and my excitement too fast
We decide to Date each other at 4 PM today
I watched the clock many times today
but the time is going very slow."
"On 3:45 PM, I reached out the Area where we will meet
These 15 minutes goes Unexpected slow motion
Some minutes later I saw a girl came to me
And what's that she is my Date."
"I am inner excited and pick her hand to reach out the destination
We move inside the Restro and people looks like our family
I thought we are Bridegroom and walk towards
the pavilion for our new life."
"We start talking with each other and telling about our Dreams
Dreams to live with each other whole the life
Dreams to make happy life with
each other."
"We don't know How the time passed away
We do many promises and talk about
the life we will going to live
with each other."
"I convinced her to Dance with me
And we doing Dance together
The Date goes to awesome
We both are serious."
"The day when we meet with each other

I will never forget and never lost
that time when we going to
be talk together."
"After 4 years of our Relationship in life
Our bonding goes to strong and
she still my life, my love
and My Girlfriend."

CHAPTER THREE

My Bestfriend Forever

I'm happy to have this wonderfull or cheerfull audience who read this Book - "One-sided Flirtinship" in front of me. Let's read the poem - "My Bestfriend Forever". Let's Begin...

Look, That's the amazing fact of my Life
I got someone who understand
my feelings from deep
of my heart.
Yes, That's the only person who understand me
and make my day wonderful and gets
all the problems what I have
to make me relax.
Oh! I forget to tell you that she the only one who
see my face when I got tensioned and I
saw herself tensioned too, when
I'm in problems.
My Life goes to much excited and wonderful
because of only her and she make my
days too much Crazy as I saw
smile on her face.
She is not just my friend but Best Friend Ever
who never take me serious but feel my
soul as we are the soulmate

just forever.
I get her in my life because I know she is the one
who only make changes in myself ever
Pick my weak points and try to
make me strongest ever.
I Love to spend my maximum time with her because
she make me feel relax and convert my
pain into the fortune which give
my Relaxation too.
Hope the Friendship never break ever and we will always
be together as a Soulmate in the future
Grow together, Live together
and Die Be Together.

CHAPTER FOUR

My School Bus

The Poem - "My School Bus" written by Gourav Paliwal was the best memories of his life. He enjoy the moments which he experience in the School Bus. Let's Begin...

Whenever I remember the days of my Schooling
I always thought about the moment
happened in the School Bus
in the childhood days.
The moments were so amazing and no one
made any non sense incident which
allowed to hurt some once
feelings.
One day, I and my friends were sit inside the bus
and suddenly some bikes stopped and
bitten on the glass of the bus
which hurt me a lots.
The good thing was that Our Teachers also travelled
with us and they were help me to overcome
from the injury which I got by
First aid procedure.
My friends were trying to go outside and fight with those
Unwanted creatures who's tried to injured me
But our teachers stopped them and
gave strict instruction.

Our Principal was also travelled with us in the Bus
He tried to talk with those idiot peoples.
But they all were start spanking
him with solid things.
Teachers called our Founder and told him whole the
Incident
Our founder sir came on the place of Incident with
Police force and they were arrested by
the Police on the spot.
When Police asked them that "Why they were do this"
then
One of them told to the Police that I was come from
Bicycle regular basis and one of my friend hired
them to killed me.
I was safe due to my School Bus because on that day
the key of my bicycle was lost and I left it in
the School to take the Bus for want to
my house easily.
The incident gave me an Exclusive story to remember
in my life and I got one more New Friend
in my Life which made my life and
that is - MY SCHOOL BUS.

CHAPTER FIVE

My Love, My Pride

*The Poem - "My Love, My Pride" is the emotional attached
with poet's emotions which he was feel about the journey
with his love or we can say his Crush. Let's Begins/...*
Whenever I saw her smile on the face
The moment is bright ever for me
I am happy she always stay
with me as shadow.
She never disappointed me in the life
Do you know Why? Because
she Love me so much
as I can do.
Love is the simple and amazing feeling ever
Love is pride and Honour to Us
Love is feeling of Pleasure
and Deep satisfaction.
When she smile then I smile too
when she sad then I sad too
when she feels happy
Yes, I happy too.
Her every moment of life is the part of my life
Her every problem is my Quiz session
Her every good opportunity is
my proud moment too.

Love has no limit to bounding In or bounding Out.

CHAPTER SIX

Time

In our life, most of the time we feel alone or afraid from something which doesn't happened but we think It's will be happen soon. To overcome this fear, The Poet write his Poem - "Time" or "Waqt". So, What are you waiting for? Let's Enjoy it.

This time every time
wanted to try me
all my existence
Why did the world
want to suppress,
Why was my mind alone
In this pretentious market,
Why is the person sold here?
In the embodiment of this wealth.
we all forget that time
changes from moment to moment,
here in the blink of an eye
Everyone's history turns
some people are
Those who are not afraid of nature,
God to some great men
There was no fear.
the atmosphere changes

Feelings change
sometimes the day changes
So sometimes the night changes,
with the help of nature
someone's alphas change,
If you ever change your mind
Sometimes thoughts change
relying on luck
Every person changes.
so is the weather
Look at the angry
God like this,
my luck is bad
So how can I convince him,
rude if someone owns
So how can I explain again,
the life that hurts me
Then how can I live?
so come together again
Let us all resolve together
on the stage of life
Fill unique colors every moment,
never hate anyone
Never fight with anyone here,
fraternally with each other
May we fill new sweetness in relationships,
all the troubles of life
Let's make it easy in a moment.

www.ingramcontent.com/pod-product-compliance
Lightning Source LLC
Chambersburg PA
CBHW022044150726
47990CB00004B/1607